TRANSAT[

Later Poems

A. L. Rowse

*Poetry is a piece of very private history
which unostentatiously lets us into the
secret of a man's life.*
– Thoreau

TABB HOUSE

First published 1989
Tabb House, 7 Church Street, Padstow, Cornwall, PL28 8BG

Printed and bound by Quintrell & Co. Ltd.
Wadebridge, Cornwall.

To
Penelope Tremayne
poet, heroic spirit

Preface

These poems of the last decade continue the themes and experiences that prevail in other volumes, brought together in *A Life: Collected Poems*: Cornwall, Oxford, America, if in different order. They cast a cold eye on the human scene, the desolation that surrounds us in the modern world, civilisation undermined by two world-wars, the consequences continuing.

In such a world solipsism is a stronghold. And one always has the consolations of the beauty of nature and landscape, the individual affections of men and animals, of memory and friendship, if not of faith.

I remain faithful to the technique that has served me all through life: regular verse alternating with irregular, traditional with free verse, plenty of rhyme internal as well as external and of alliteration natural to natural poets.

Contemporary poetry is in as much confusion as the contemporary world and exhibits the same deterioration of standards: often utter formlessness, lack of pattern as of thought – at its best, the material for poetry, not the thing itself. Educated and trained poets, like Eliot and Betjeman, Auden and Larkin, thought little of it; and Spender asks the pertinent question whether the poets of the past would recognise modernist 'verse' as poetry at all.

A. L. R.

Contents

The Conveyor-Belt

Here I am on the conveyor-belt,
Not to get off until my fate's made clear,
The plan fulfilled invoking America,
Myself subjected to necessity.
Still here as yet tumultuous breakers gnaw
At the south coast of Devon, sea reddened
By blood of the cliffs, pock-marked, pitted by spume.
Even the sheltered estuary's angry
Under a leaden sky, papered by gulls.
No flag flies over Powderham today,
The secular Devons given up and gone away,
And Nutwell Court no longer inhabited
By descendants of the Drakes beside the Exe.
A century – an epoch's at an end
And all I care for relics of the past,
Relegated, thrown aside, forlorn.
I set my face towards another world –
No stirring of the heart, nor love, nor hope,
But duty, stern daughter of necessity.

Leaving Cornwall for U.S.A.

Primroses cluster the railway cuttings
Daffodils dally in valley bottoms
Wind in osiers, sedges, willows
The stripling Fowey goes rippling gaily
Pyramid larches spire horizons
A road marches up to moorland
Cloudscape lours on villages, vistas
Clearings in rhododendron copses
On mottled cattle in primeval mud.
Hither and thither the heather weather
Marks the slopes of china clay burrows
The plough shapes the hilly landscapes
Punctuated by sheep cropping
Till now come Trematon and Tamar
The Hamoaze and its mirrored windshield
River beds, tides, estuaries
Cut the land into a thousand figures:
Curves and contours speak to heart's blood
More than the myriad works of man.

Jumbo Jet

In this plane I'm just a parcel,
No longer an individual soul;
The minute of tension, the moment of take-off
Is over, and all is yet in control.

In this jumbo jet of latest design
Three hundred such human parcels are we;
Flight is westward along with the sun,
The plane crowded to capacity.

But suppose if the plane loses height,
In course of landing goes out of control:
Will each of the three hundred parcels
Rate an individual soul?

Transatlantic

While over snow-bound, rock-ribbed Labrador
A Texan fist-fight occupies the screen –
Houston or Dallas of evil memory,
Desert, sandy wastes, palms, the ring,
Backers watching as excited as we.
Sombreros and cops' helmets, cowboy hats
Crowd background and keep the ring, and that's
How they and we pass the declining day.
Their belly-laughs our normal kids reveal,
Nothing to reflect, nothing to conceal,
Euphoric, unconstrained and innocent,
Given over to unaffected merriment,
Inane guffaws at features on the screen
As if such things before they'd never seen:
A car-chase, the police in hot pursuit,
Hip to hip, whichever is first to shoot,
Who is victim, who the guilty one
In this good-humoured exhibition –
Bruises, smiles, patches over the eye,
Their girls as cheer-leaders, looking on:
Later, the bar, drinks around the saloon.
A mule looks down superciliously
At the exposure of human vacuity.

At Bowdoin College, Maine

'Alpheus Spring Packard, for sixty five years
A loyal member of the faculty of the College.'
One sees an old-fashioned gentleman, springy and spare
As it might be a Lawrence Lowell or Christian Gauss,
Handle-bar moustaches, devoted to his young men,
Yet prim and reserved, not giving himself away
To sharp-eyed dowagers in that innocent day
And time, a celibate from the Civil War . . .
The visit over, evening and quiet, fragrance
Of resin in pines, scent of leaves on ground,
Of leaves burning off-campus; student noises,
Wireless, light tenor voices, day's work over;
Light filtered on tree trunks, on eager young faces
Running to Hall; verdant vistas darken
As shadows close. – As shadows close on the man
Observing youth and the morning play of life,
Gold hair that grows grey, runners whose pace will slow –
Pride and flourish of youth, the stalwart stride,
Vigour of baseball player, track-runner in shorts –
All will yet become one with the greener shades
Of former evenings, and those formerly here.

The Senator

———————

'So Maud is dead. She was a good little whore',
Said the Senator for Pennsylvania
To the Madam – no Quaker State humbug for him.
Though fifth generation in America,
He never once wore a tuxedo, but knew
The saloons and brothels of Philadelphia,
The pavements and the bars with their spittoons.
He had no use for democracy, but bought
The people's votes. Himself was not for sale:
An aristo and rich, he bribed others.
One private vice he had: he collected rare books,
Was well-read in early literature.
That would not have won him any votes.

On his yacht on the Delaware one day,
A giant of six foot four, equally obese,
He stood on deck, naked as the day he was born,
Well equipped, well hung. A lady guest
Feigned surprise and shock, as women will,
Thinking it due to female modesty.
'If you see anything you haven't seen before,
Then you should be ashamed of yourself', said he.
He died, not of drink or syphilis, as you
Might expect, but just from over-eating.

———————

Campus Amenities

———————

Bursts of forsythia explode the winter,
Octopus arms reaching up to sun;
Bridal wreath breaks white and shy
Under the lucid Virginian sky.
Sparks of raindrops appear
Diamonds on dogwood and juniper;
Violets leap out of the improbable earth,
Débris of winter, sticks like snakes lie
Across the lawn, alive with squirrels.
Above, their gurgitations grate
Against bark of trees, as the bleat
Of students predicates a mate.
In the mornings patient didacticism,
In the evenings radio and communal noise
Prevail with graduated eroticism:
Acquiescent girls lead on the boys.
The campus tart with predatory eye
Approaches the alien don:
'What are you doing, while here, for fun?'

A carillon chimes the hour of evensong:
In this cold climate no song is sung.

———————

The Pavements of Pasadena

With what heart-ache I walked
The pavements of Pasadena,
A sad self-willed exile.
There were the trim palings,
Pretty lawns and parterres,
Oleander, hibiscus,
Clouds of morning glory
Trailing over doorways
With starred clematis.
Up towards Altadena
Evening lights begin,
Pinpoint the boulevards,
Patterning the slopes.
Down here in windows
Friendly lights reveal
Domestic life within.
The exile pauses a moment,
Foot poised on pavement,
Savours the expectation
Of someone home returning
From the day's chores in town,
Family life gathering –
Pauses and peers, a stranger
To happy comfort of heart.
Looks, then passes on,
Always and ever outside.

Commemoration

We commemorate a life now closed
Here in late reluctant Virginian spring;
The friendly folk all gathered in
Here to recall a life well-lived within
The marked-out margins of this neighbourhood,
Pin-oak, deodar and cottonwood.
The chaste and spare chapel windows speak
Of days of the Georges and the Old Dominion.
A different inflexion now prevails:
No Mass, nor priest to celebrate –
Young people to hand round the elements
Of bread and wine in secular seemliness,
Unconsecrated. And so in neighbourliness
We all partake – one, more touched at heart
For want of faith than those to whom these things
Are of the daily round unsanctified.
Thus can I drown an eye unused to flow
For precious friends hid in death's dateless night –
Here recalled this sullen Sunday morning
So far from home, so many years ago
Now I'm grown old; while they remain still young,
Brought back in mind at this memorial
For an unknown spirit in a different land.

Known Only to God

―――――――――

'The whole Agatha', I believe,
Is known only to God',
She writes. And is this true?
And is this true also for me?
I do not know. I cannot believe,
But would it were so.
This happy Sunday morning
On my sun-porch in Virginia,
Daffodils out, forsythia, mahonia,
Chinese bamboos that beckon and wave
– And I am almost at home.
Almost – as much at home as anywhere,
And yet for ever outside,
Never giving myself
To anyone, perhaps least of all
To God.

―――――――――

The Absent One

A month ago
All here was snow,
The garden a pall of white:
But now behold
Blue, rose and gold
For your and my delight.

Birds on the wing
Announce the Spring
And sing out over the Meadow:
Over the wall
Blossoms fall,
On all the green no shadow.

A peal of bells
Across the air tells
Me that May has come:
That you're never here
Fills me with fear.
O echoing bells, be dumb!

Cartmel Bells

———————

O Cartmell bells ring soft tonight,
   And Cartmel bells ring clear,
Though I lie far away tonight
   Listening with my dear.

Listening in a frosty land
   Where all the bells are still,
And small the windowed towers stand
   Dark under heath and hill.

———————

No *Redintegratio Amoris*

It was the last time I ever saw you –
Background of a cathedral and a Queen –
I thought all was repaired between us
And that we would resume relations,
If not on the old footing of love,
At least on the warm foothold of friendship.

I hoped in vain. It was not to be:
Cold, inexplicable silence followed –
As if there had been no friendliness or gaiety
In meeting on ground sacred to memory'
Of your youth and grace, spontaneity
And happiness in mutual embrace.

I could not comprehend it. Had someone intervened,
Censored our contact, forbidden friendship?
Or was it casual charm that reassured me
That all was well, when it was not?
The heart-ache continued, the void
Where once there had been
Love.

Sex in May

———————

Maytime sultriness and sex
Young men lie under the wisteria
Formerly frequented by you
No longer a visitant summer or winter –
The insatisfaction of summer
Holding the wolf of sex at bay
While the young are in erotic play.
The scents of hawthorn and balsam poplar
Drug the drowsy senses with delight
While a summer wind frills the white
World of wild parsley in flower
Petals strew the speckled path
The grass verge laid by the late shower.
Sunday families all in their best
After their pleasure recover their breath
Along the river where the red oars sway
Under a similar rhythm –
The rhythm of reproduction and of life
Held for this moment of day
At bay.

———————

The North-West

Why is the North-West so mysterious?
Why does it move me so?
Somehow places a cold touch
On mind and heart,
And yet so beautiful?
Is it the billowing white clouds –
Angel-heads I thought as a child?
Or the refraction of sun
That casts a numb eye
On trees and open sky?
Yet it is none of these:
It is some way of seeing the world
I cannot express –
Something withdrawn that not invites,
Some perfection inaccessible
To the mind and hope of man.

On Richard Strauss's *Metamorphosen*

Grief, *immer weinend, weinend* –
The downward sweep of strings,
The restless uncertainty, seeking,
Seeking some assurance of security.
There is none.
Save perhaps in haunting memory
Of what has been in happier days –
No base, nothing but disgrace,
Nothing to uphold the soul.
The bitter strings rise to shrill
Protest at the world's insanity,
The insanity of those who create not,
Nor do they spin fine webs of sound –
Like these that search the heart
With remembered happiness,
For consolation in despair.

What consolation in the world's despair?

O hoher Baum im Ohr –
None but the spirits
Who construct an inner world
Of secret joy to counter outer ill.
After long wandering in polyphony
Resolution is reached in lyric constancy:
A world in ruins has its elegy.

The Family Pew

Sitting in church in the family pew
Where I first set eyes on them: two girls
Just setting out on life, as indeed was I
At back of the church, under their scrutiny
The start of a long story
Of life's journey now drawing to an end.
Play the game of Supposes – suppose
If it had come about and two of us
Had joined our fate and fortune for the journey?
Instead of which they made sad marriages,
While I made my *maladif* way alone.

Fifty years after, promoted to the pew,
We repeat the remembered petitions of Morning Prayer:
We have erred and strayed like lost sheep –
As it might be on the seaward slopes of Stoke,
In the violet combes of Speke's Mill Mouth,
The up-ended sarcophagi of Hartland Quay.
And I awake from mnemonic dream to see
I am shouldering the memorial of one
Younger than I, yet twenty years dead:
Gallant Captain in the Guards, who served
Throughout the war; shared the bachelor house
At Buscot with American friend,
Died in the train, and so the line had end.

But suppose it had been otherwise?
At the bend of the river towards Annery
When I halt by the roadside to remember her
Looking upstream to Wear Giffard, I think of the fun –
Contingent and intermittent for me –
When we were young, and all was yet to be.
But would it have done?

Or suppose I had been his friend
Who loved his lineal Hartland, often came
Here for holiday, who now rests –
Where? Not here. Leaving only a name
On a plaque as benefactor of the place:
Which moves me strangely who hardly knew
Him whose presence fills the familiar pew.

———————

The Wise Man of Restormel

On the hill the Wise Man lives
  Overlooking the sleepy town,
Comfort, strength and healing gives
  To all and sundry, up and down

The river valley; all the way
  From Lanhydrock to the sea at Fowey,
Restormel to Boconnoc Park,
  He cures the ills that much annoy

Animals and men alike:
  Scurvy and ringworm, warts on hands,
Corns and chilblains, goitre, growths
  On throat and neck that threaten glands.

Words a few he will recite,
  Sign with cross, mumble a charm:
Shortly the evil vanishes,
  At length diminishes the harm.

Wise with ancient folklore knowing,
  Wisdom long likely to endure,
Stricken in years, uncertain of health,
  His own disease he cannot cure.

Treffry's[1] Viaduct

These are the roads I loved to walk –
Up Minear Lane to Carn Grey,
Trethurgy and across Sterrick Moor,
In heat of summer or autumn day:

Up here it's always clean and cool
With moorland scents and tang of air,
Past the turning to Methrose
Within its granite bounds. And there

In Georgian days John Wesley stayed
With faithful friends, the farming Knights,
Preached and prayed, and took some rest
In his laborious days and nights.

On to Luxulyan, now not far,
Grey tower beside its screen of trees.
Down three steps into the aisle,
Within the walls I take my ease

Before descent into the Valley
Beside the limpid brown trout stream –
To rest beneath the Viaduct:
Imperial expression of a dream

In stone, Regency and Roman,
Soaring high into the sky.
Admire the genius of the man
Conceived and builded it – Treffry.

---

1. The name is pronounced with the accent on the second syllable.

The Road to Penrice

———————

Along the road a screen of oaks
   Sturdy and strong used to be here,
Beside the deer-park of Penrice –
   Now vanished like the deer.

When we were young and hopes were high
   We took our walks along this way –
Porthpean, the ledra at Trenarren,
   The winding lanes above the bay:

Hedges full of ragged robin,
   Rust-red sorrel and rest-harrow,
Golden kingcups, wild snapdragon
   Flowered the byway to Pencarrow.

So, on to the turning to Polglaze,
   The agèd elms that spread their fan
Have vanished like the oaks, the deer –
   And we, like them, will soon have done.

———————

At Charlestown

(for David Treffry)

A gibbous moon through the enchanted copse
And lighted eyes of a house on the cliff,
A rain cloud rolls away to the west,
Leaving the high skyline free.
The dark brushwork of browse below
Telegraph wires on the horizon,
Venus above – and you on the North-West Frontier,
The river scenes of Kashmir. Here
Ominous black waters under the cliff:
The sense of the poignancy of life
Awakens echoes in the heart
As a whistle blows – and childhood
Comes back in the arrested moment.
Duporth bell chimes out mutability,
Life's transitory fragility.

The Road to the Nare

We rose up with the dawn of day
And filled our lungs with summer air,
Along the lanes we went our way
And set our faces to the Nare.

We passed the white gate at Penrice
And on the left we left Trenarren,
By twisted tracks and paths we went
And so descended to Pentewan.

The sun was high, the sea wind soft,
We stepped it out that cloudless day –
While all the morning at our feet
Lay the mapped waters of the bay.

Before us on the high skyline
Gorran tower we kept in view,
Past Pencarrow and Polglaze,
A turning to the right – St Ewe.

The honeysuckle hedges leaned
Over us on either hand,
Foxgloves, scabious, purple vetches
Coloured all the scented land.

At evening, when the sun went down,
The rose-flush in the western skies
And starry points of lighted gorse
Mingled with starlight in our eyes.

Marika at Maidenwell

Whose is that spirit moving over the Moor,
So light of heart and step, so full
Of the poet's 'courage, love, and joy'?
Leaping from Stripple Stones to Altarnun,
Over the Moor from Colliford to Rowtor.
What is that hill up which she used to go,
Flare of skirt and eyes, to Carburrow? –
Cloudscape, snowscape, map of men's minds,
On the horizon the heave of breast of Caradon.
Keeping open house, open heart, compelling
Generosity – for ever cooking, creating
Dishes: salmon from the Warleggan river,
Frying Helford oysters up from Port Navas,
Mushrooming along the fringes of the woods,
Or down by the cavern where the adders live –
She had no fear of them but held them friends,
And found no adders among human kind.
What joy in life, skating on Dozmary,
Chartering a plane to dine in Corsica;
Accompanying Robin up the Amazon
To the inaccessible hearts of Stone Age men.

A shadow crosses the land by Treverbyn Vean,
Informs the variegated colours of the woods,
Comes to rest at length by the living waters,
The haunted spring of Maidenwell.

The Dead Lady

The lovely lady is dead,
Her loving spirit fled –
Whither we do not know,
There is nothing to show
For those beautiful eyes,
Generous, kind and wise,
The gaiety beneath
The constant threat of death.
So tenuous a hold
On life – nothing bold,
But brave to endure
Life's ills: a spirit pure
With no common taint;
The frail integument
Of flesh now broken, shed
Like a cast garment – free
To confront the mystery
Ever in life concealed,
Now to her revealed?

Tullimar, Perranworthal

(*For William Golding*)

Melancholy moment at Tullimar
Of the old Princess: summer rain
Like tears on Regency façade –
Formal fuchsias, informal hydrangeas,
White agapanthus and magnolia,
Cherry trees and urns, the welcoming portico
To the Napoleonic presence, the Malmaison tent.
Mist over the valley from Restronguet,
The creek where the ships came up
With Norwegian spruce and fir, pit-props
For the mines no longer working –
No longer the bearded, ear-ringed sailors,
The girls waiting for them by the quay.
Not even a quay any more, the fairway
Filled with sand, the ships laid up.
No longer a Princess to welcome me.

Tregeare

(For Charles Causley)

Tregeare – how lonely stands the gaunt house,
The last member of the family gone.
The house stands tall and shuttered,
Blind windows that once opened
Across shaved and level lawn
To distant Bodmin Moor on summer horizon.

The meet would be here on dewy mornings,
Red coats gay on their mounts, sleek horses,
The hounds impatient to be gone over moor
And field and stream. The family would come
Out on the terrace, stand on the columned porch
Dispensing hospitality, become impossible:
Farms sold one by one, things folding up,
Life slowing down.
In lush Victorian days, sons home from India,
Not a weed would show in the forecourt,
Where the stable clock stands at twenty to three.
So it has stood for twenty years. Dorothy's
Thatched summer house, where she played
Games as a girl, now falling in together –
Peer down the walks, the unkempt drive,
Rhododendron and camellia interlaced
With strangling brambles, nettles, bindweed.

And yet, O once, in early May the mountain
Of purple ponticum would put forth its glory:
The cedar summon the shades to tea in its shadow,
A footman to bring it, châtelaine in bombazine
To preside over friendly group at table –
Where today all is emptiness and vacancy.
The gate clangs behind the trespasser
Upon all this shuttered life. And still
Stands the stable clock at twenty to three.

The Face in the Nave

———————

In the church the people gathered
    To celebrate harvest festival –
Sheaves of corn on ledge and sill,
    Fruits and flowers, gourds and all

Offerings from the country round,
    Orchard and garden, field and meadow.
Suddenly on a pillar of nave
    Two women saw appear a shadow

That shortly formed into a face,
    A countenance of evil that
Made them shrink with horror, and
    Stifle a cry of fear thereat.

What was the shape both saw together?
    What apparition could it have been?
– Long ago, in the Civil War,
    A captain of Cromwell's had then seen

Fit to set alight the store
    Of gunpowder beneath the tower.
That day was the anniversary:
    This was the man and this the hour.

———————

Last of the Line

I've often thought of that old Devon name
And the young fellow who came to say goodbye –
Not handsome, but erect and stalwart, fine
In his new uniform, standing by
My door, not saying much, perhaps proud
Of his family name descended to yeoman stock,
Aware of what was expected of it
In all the earlier vanished centuries.

There he stood, ready in heavy kit
For embarkation at once for service abroad.
Little was said between us:
Some strange taciturnity
Held us both, and something was on his mind.
Why had he come to me to say goodbye?
He was going into the line, and perhaps
He knew he'd not come back.
Did he wish me to know that he was doing his duty
Expected by his folk, that I would know,
As he left my room, he was the last of the line?

'The Haven'

He had come through the years at war,
And clearly liked it very well:
All set fair for happiness –
All unexpected what befell.

Contented with his battery
And his belovèd chestnut mare,
Riding twenty miles a day –
Fought at Mons and Festubert.

'This is war, and no mistake –
 Still it's grand to be out here';
Wounded once and again, then back
To the Line to give the lads a cheer:

A happy family – as at home,
The selfsame spirit when a boy,
Rowing the Red Boat over the river,
Sailing out from the haven of Fowey.

Now riding through the fields of Flanders,
Honeysuckle, broom, wild flowers,
Cornflowers, poppies red as blood;
The moon comes up – what scented hours!

'We sleep by a barn that's full of hay,
Yet still I long for a sight of the sea' –
Then 'the deafening noise of the guns',
The danger, the camaraderie.

On leave in Paris with his girl,
Gallant ribbons on his chest,
There they make their plans to marry –
'And, after all, love is best'.

Armistice comes: in Nôtre Dame
A thousand candles light the nave,
Before each one a figure in black
Kneels and prays, remembers a grave.

'When we lived in holes in the ground',
He said, 'we never caught a chill';
The war over, and all secure
When in the Rhineland he fell ill.

Gulls on the house, a smell of the sea –
When life at last seemed safe and well:
'Dearest, we shall come home', he wrote.
Out of clear sky the blow fell.

———————

Sailor Boy in the Train

Bell–bottomed sailor, O beauty
   With gold ring in your ear,
What will time take from you
   As year succeeds to year?

You slope down the corridor,
   Enter the door with grace;
Each of us makes room for you,
   Eyes drawn to your face.

Red cliffs of your native Devon
   And golden gorse flash by,
Blue of sea and blue of sky
   Reflected in your eye:

A modern Raleigh without pride,
   But natural dignity;
The youthful, curling, copper beard
   Attests virility.

The women's glances feed on you
   Unconscious and innocent –
Perhaps as yet not quite aware
   Of sexual intent.

But what will the years do to you,
   Roll on in their disgrace:
Family burdens, and the scars
   Of age on mind and face.

Trafalgar Square

Behold this quarry of human history,
Or, rather, of an empire at an end.
Nelson aloft against October cloud and sky,
Beneath, the monuments of the nation's past,
Disjecta membra of a happier time.
Here is Napier, 'erected by public subscription,
The most numerous of them being private soldiers';
Here Havelock, of the Indian Mutiny,
Commanding Oude Irregulars, Bengal Engineers,
Madras Fusiliers and Highland Foot.
The brightly striped and saaried Indian girls
Are being photographed beneath the hero:
All the flotsam and jetsam from the once
Gorgeous East, turbaned and camera-hung.

Tread softly, for you tread on my dreams,
Or on the congregated pigeons sober
As in church, here and there one flies up
On a fancier's shoulder, not however on mine.
The present holds no honour for me, only
The dream of the past, this graveyard of monuments,
Fossils of a more glorious, more amusing
Clime. The absurd Regent prances on horse,
The columns of his vanished Carlton House
For background, looks vacantly at Nelson.
Did this Regent of fantasy think that he
Was at Trafalgar? What would Nelson reply?
Turn a blind eye to the wheeling sky?

St Martin's steeple chimes a quarter to four:
A pallid sun peeps out to light the page,
The moving finger of time that writes, the man
Himself but a shadow column of his age.
Look down Whitehall, to the vista of Big Ben
And the former Mother of Parliaments: no future
There. Look down the once imperial way,
As the melancholy fated king looks down,
Contemplates his own last tragic day.

October sun runs up the fluted column,
And it is Trafalgar Day. Nelson is lost,
Far removed from the reeling world below:
A world in dissolution and decay,
The demos at ease, and everywhere out of control.

———————

Trafalgar Day in Madron Church

———————

Under the lee of St Michael's Mount
   A Newlyn fisherman in the Bay
Encountered the dispatch-boat *Pickle*
   Bringing news upon her way

Up-Channel – of a glorious victory,
   But sealed and saddened by the death
Of the nation's hero in self-same hour:
   In death as in life he kept the faith.

Sheltering from storm and wind,
   The ship lit up by angry sun,
Flame and crimson as the blood
   Spilt on deck ere that day was done.

In Chapel Street the Assembly Rooms
   Filled with the good folk of Penzance
Gay in the flickering candlelight
   Paused in the middle of the dance,

When the Mayor aloft in the gallery
   Called for silence to announce
The glorious yet grievous news . . .
   A hush fell on the crowd. At once

With one impulse the gathering poured
   Out in the street above the Bay,
Up the hill to Madron church
   There to give thanks, and grieve and pray

For all the fallen along with him.
   And every year, as if time should stay,
The faithful gather there in church
   Still to remember Trafalgar Day.

———————

Looks

I shut my eyes against the ugliness
Of humans – male and female created He them
No matter – when it comes to looks all's one.
Drink deforms the face of the naval man,
The prominent dog-teeth of the woman next,
Ill-tempered corners of a mouth turned down;
That one's hair a tangled bird's nest,
Irregular eyes and ears, and pendant nose.
How rarely one sees a countenance to rest on –
Like the sailor boy at Euston going North,
Quite unaware of what drew eyes towards him:
Perfection in the brief prime of youth.

Look out of the window at the landscape rather,
Pastoral green and golden leaves of autumn,
Occasional sun on wood and wold and field,
Offering relief from the disgrace
Of the human scene, body, limb and face.

The Human Factor
(For Graham Greene)

The traveller to Malayan war observes:
Scotch planter and wife drive in to Kuala Lumpur
For St Andrew's day dinner; they reach the haggis when
News is brought them of their infant daughter
Shot point-blank by Communists.
Thus was the Party Catechism carried out:
'The Party has resolved the question of love'.

Lunatic hunger-strikers kill themselves
For what they think a principle –
For marching morons down Fifth Avenue,
Shouting slogans of martyrdom.

The visiting reporter still remembers
'The sharp image of the dead child couched
In the dusty ditch beside dead mother:
The neatness of the bullet wounds
More disturbing than the general massacre
In the canals around, to discriminating eye'.

'The Sinister Spirit sneered, "It had to be",
And again the Spirit of Pity whispered, "Why?"'
No pity for animal or man –
In the universe: only in the minds of some
Men, the universe itself being neutral
To our suffering. God said not a hair
Of man's head shall be hurt, He is cognisant
Of the fall of every sparrow from the heaven.

'From outside the hut you could not see within
The woman's charred corpse, the body robbed of entrails,
The child cut in two halves across the waist,
The officer still living with lower jaw
Sliced off, with one hand, one foot severed.'

And God shall wipe away all tears from their eyes;
And there shall be no more death, neither sorrow, nor crying;
Neither shall there be any more pain:
For the former things are passed away.

All God's l'il chillun got wings, with their oaths
In blood, their Mau-Mau ceremonies
With living sheep, dead goat, and naked woman –
'The forced circumcision of the girls,
The white farmer hacked open in his bath,
The little boy cut to pieces on his bed
Beside his toys, his diminutive railway track.'

What are these which are arrayed in white robes?
And whence came they? These are they which came
Out of great tribulation, and have washed their robes
And have made them white in the blood of the Lamb.

Here upon the universe
Is the curse: Nature red in tooth and claw,
Man a part of Nature no less, but worse.
Poison in the fangs of snakes; sea-snakes
Project a hundred times more powerful venom
Upon their prey to paralyse the victim;
The raven or carrion crow that will peck out
The eyes of overturned, defenceless sheep;
Kite or owl or jay that will strike down
An innocent small creature, a few feathers
Upon the path to indicate a kill.
The lion roaring after his prey doth seek
His meat from God.

                    Such a universe
So created can not be understood
By the puny mind of man, not large enough
To grasp the pattern, contradictions of mood
In such creative ecstasy; nor so
Insensitive to the suffering of every
Created thing throughout it all, to deny
Its Creator pity – if Creator indeed be.

Suburbia

They have mouths, and speak not:
eyes have they, and see not. They
have ears, and hear not: noses have
they, and smell not.
                    Psalm 115

Look at the idiot people at their games –
I see them as so many baboons in a zoo,
Their own local zoo among the tenements,
A patch graceless as a monkey's bare behind:
Playing games of moving chairs about,
Standing in self-conscious attitudes
To catch each other in the eye of the camera –
As in the cold eye of the observer in the train,
Watching their infant idiosyncracies.
Now one comes up behind another to put
Arms around bulging breasts or hips,
Unselfconscious, unknowing, unaware:
Slaves of nature, just like other animals,
Copulating, conceiving, giving birth,
Their own animals but simulacra of them.
See the summer acreage of ugly flesh,
The borborygmic joys of family life!
Not one observes the beauty of the world,
The panoply of may along the river banks,
Explosions of golden gorse and broom
Amid the arrested suburban greenery,
Chestnuts coming into flower, and lilac
Above the squalor of the human scene.
Nor notice that the honeysuckle's out.

Married Happiness

I am haunted by an image from my youth
A girl leans over her garden gate as I pass,
Golden haired, blue-eyed and dimpled
I remembered her as a boy from my schooldays –
Now married. She has her man in the background –
Mystery lurks in his masculine sex,
Dark and lean, silent as a fox.
She, all contentment, arms spread wide
Leans over the gate, the kindly superior smile
Of a few years older at the growing youth,
Never initiated into the secret of life.
A golden radiance from the harvest moon
Bathes all the valley – Boscoppa, Bethel:
Each awaits the happy moment for bed,
Expectation in her eyes, he darkly watching her.
Having understood,
The youth goes on his way
In accustomed solitude.

Village Life

I walk through the village in a trance of TV,
Proud as a paycock: people turn out to see
The boy who made good. But while they look at me
They are not what's in my eye. Those I see
Are all gone, fifty years gone into the earth
With their sadness and mirth. Old Enas Kellow and wife,
The neighbours would listen in at their strife,
She thirty years older, and a proper scarecrow.
Monkey-brand Rowe, with his dark frizzled daughter
'Desidered 'ansome an' demired be 'underds', he said;
The son turned out as a masher, two kid gloves
And one to carry, a cane to flourish in the hand.

An old sea-captain would rise early to scour
The fields for mushrooms before anybody was up,
Lodged with morose Miss Pope and her love-child,
Pretty May Pope, at last made her mother Mrs Taylor.
Over at end of the village the ill-omened farm,
The Duchy farm, where the farmer went mad,
Threatened to kill wife and children. He ended in the Asylum.

What a life was there, what a crowded canvas!
Sexy Bill Dustow exposed an enormous tool,
Beery ex-sailor, to the woman across the way,
And introduced the growing boys to sex no less.
Not that, next door, Miss Ham, we called her Mrs, needed it:
With her pal Lucy, of the blazing eyes –
She was the town prostitute: on market nights
Sallied down to the pubs, a one-arm disguised by cape,
To make her living by pick-ups for the week-end.
And in the end the poor soul died of syphilis.

Hot-gospeller, club-foot tailor Freeman,
Mad-languaged from the Book of Revelation,
Wife's mind turned each month with change of the moon
Would quarrel with the neighbour next door –
We saw them fight, each pulling the other's hair.
Annie Courtney, 'black as a Zulu', they said –
Had she gipsy blood? – left the village
Where she had spent her life, to join
Daughter in Detroit, and die far from home, thinking
At the last she heard the church bells ring –
As they rang for us, Sunday morning and evening.

Instead of day, I see the dusk descend,
The street lamp lit, the lads come out to play
Ball against the shop's expanse of wall
Till night shuts up the shop.
I see it all.

———————————

Mrs Manrow

Mrs Manrow, like a mandril with blue bum,
Sits in her drawing room
Waiting for her guests to come.
She has daughters four
To marry off – no time to lose.
A gathering of collegers
Is bidden, and of them
The most eligible and select.
Politely around the Bechstein grand,
While the girls perform, they stand,
Cups of tea in balanced hand.
While she surveys the young men's looks,
Mrs Manrow discusses books,
The latest come up for review
Before down the stairs the couples vanish –
Perhaps, then, *The Bridge of San Luis Rey?*
Undefeated Mrs Manrow would say,
'Oh, yes: I read it in the original Spanish.'

All Souls Day

_____

Justorum animae in manu dei sunt.
Brightly, warmly descends the autumn sun
On the morning chapel, and it is All Souls day.
The shadow of a bird passes up the painted
Glass, even as our lives in time will pass –
Colours on reredos and rows of the dead,
Amethyst and saffron, rose, blue, green.
Here they are gathered in mind who all are gone.

The ancient Warden reads the Founder's prayer,
Silvery hair, grey eyes, clean-shaven face,
His 'Pembers' a tuft of hair on each suave cheek.
Sermon by Henson, of beetling eyebrows
And clacking teeth, hissing across to Lang
How his predecessor at Durham, 'Analogy' Butler,
Had refused the primacy for 'he would not be
A pillar of a declining Church': on me
Not lost, for he wanted the see of York.
Old Oman whom Henson reproved for being late,
'Not only for the General Confession but
The Absolution you most stand in need of.'

Quavering-voiced, sharp-tongued Johnson, chaplain
And hunting parson, who closed discussion with
'Never ask for anything, never refuse anything,
And never resign anything' – wrestling with Morrah's
Soul, bent on going over to Rome:
Whose panegyric Reggie Harris preached
Improbably in Westminster Cathedral.
Reggie moves out, birdlike, head on one side:
I think of his jokes,
Handel, 'the great master of the common chord',
Carcassonne, 'Violé par Le Duc.'

They all move up in seniority
To make their offering at the altar.

44

Robertson, sharp of nose and kind of heart,
Loquacity his only vice. And now
Comes Geoffrey Dawson of the *Times*,
Of fatal influence on foreign policy,
With his friend the 'Prophet' Curtis, who had
A message for the world, but lost his way.
Another wounded by loss in a later war.

Behold Spencer Wilkinson in spats
Shuffling with myopic gait up the steps,
Who'd have one think he had enjoyed the favours
Of Sarah Bernhardt: soft of heart:
A military man, marsh-mallow within.
McGregor, muttering to himself, having
Been blown up on the Menin Road –
That earlier war,
Began the ruin of the age in which we live.

Woodward served in Salonica; see him
With sceptical smile and clerical trail,
Approach the communion rail.
Bridges, of frosty eye and intellect,
Secrets of state well down 'in the deep, deep freeze'.

Pares, at whose election the Warden dreamed
Primus inter pares:
On whose beloved head cruel fate
Fell, unable to move muscle or limb.
Summer afternoons we'd sit beneath
The whitebeam's canopy and watch the sky
Wheeling over battlement and spire,
While time ate up the precious hour.

They all served Church or State in their day
Who now are here, shrouded in surplices
As once they were, and now are ghosts, alive
Only in the dedicated mind.
November sunlight flickers across the aisle,
Falls upon stall and altar, whereon
The candles shed their flame, and it is written:
The souls of the just are in the hand of God.

45

Cosmo Lang, Archbishop

Coming over Shotover at Easter time,
Larks in the air, all spring down the dingles
And in the blue folds of the hills,
Suddenly he heard the call:
Another Paul on the road to Damascus.

The world stood still at that command,
Unexpected, unwanted, that yet compelled.
With inner dismay he went his way
From that high place, along the spine of land
Into the city, to accept the call to obey.

And ever after, in that dedicated life,
'Intolerable, unbearable, inevitable' –
At Easter time he returned for renewal
Of vocation to Shotover, for spiritual
Strength – hoping to hear again the voice
In all the pride and promise of spring,
Birds singing from green coverts,
Willows waving tassels in sun and wind –
The command once heard that urged him on his way.

Ghosts

Catmint, tobacco plant, roses,
And ghosts that haunt this place – encloses
Antinous with strigil in one hand
Displaying buttocks and small stand of penis
In profile to unregarding sparrows
Playing in the clematis.
Silence and suspense. The chestnut tree
Of my ambitious youth still looks at me
As if sentient, conscious and aware.
The ghosts, presences that should be here –
But are they here? or not, if not, where?
Or nowhere at all? Yet I see their faces:
Dear Richard, and bird-like Reggie,
Absent-minded Geoffrey
Incurring no less absent-mindedly
Now forgotten paternity:
Remembered still by me
This vacant hour, wondering where
They are, whither gone, or only
Alive in the observant lonely
Mind only.

Max and Agatha

Across the cornfields beaten down by rain
Cholsey church-tower stands sturdy on the dead.
And there my friends lie, Max and Agatha,
Together now – nor were in life divided
Till she lay here a few years earlier:
Leaving him, the same bright merry eye
That looked on life with kindly happiness,
Courage and spirit that led him to his end.
Now thunderclouds sweep over the tower, light up
The loved landscape by Thames and Wallingford.
The rain pours down and penetrates their graves –
The strangeness of their story the eerie light
Reminds me of, illumines their last home.

James Elroy Flecker

O see the sad expression of the eyes:
The animal looks out from carapace
Envisaging the death to be –
'I am afraid to think about my death' –
Full-lipped sensuality
Still expressive of desire,
Black thick hair full of vitality
Heavy masculine moustache
Remembers the lips of the young scholar
Avid of pots and sherds, intaglios,
Cameos, gems and figurines,
Deserting you for them, while you
Arms folded, spirit self-contained,
By life consumed, defeated
Await your end.

Lines for William Shakespeare

Reading in a book I came upon the words
In some dull prose, 'Thou hast nor youth nor age
But, as it were, an after-dinner's sleep
Dreaming on both.' The words leaped from the page:
Surprised, I suddenly found myself in tears.
There was that voice, the very rhythm and accent,
Simple, familiar, yet unmistakable,
Reaching across the yet unnumbered years,
The centuries, to touch the waiting heart.
And now again he says, 'There's no art
To find the mind's construction in the face.'
But in the magical mastery of phrase
That reaches the hidden crevices of guilt,
Remorse for what is irremediable,
That strips away pretence, hypocrisy,
The blindness to what we've done, and bares the wound.
One can hardly bear to look – a scene in a play
No longer, but the truth of life itself:
The bitter words of Hamlet to his love,
Because he loves, but believes he is betrayed;
Macbeth's wife, walking in her sleep,
Washing her hands, but blood will not away.
Leontes looks upon the ruin of his life,
Reconciled, forgiveness at the last.
Lear to the daughter he had disowned,
'Your sisters have, as I do remember, done
Me wrong. You have some cause; they have not.'
To which Cordelia: 'No cause, no cause.'
'The odds is gone, and there is nothing left
Remarkable beneath the visiting moon.'
Such words sear the heart, and search the brain.
There never has been anyone like him.

The Dying Poet

The last day the old poet was alive
He kept asking for Shakespeare's *Cymbeline*,
Tried in vain to hold it up to read.
At length 'I've opened it,' he sighed and said,
'Hang there like fruit, my soul, till the tree die.'
The moon rose, shone full into the room,
Nor did the dying poet take away
His hand from the open book that lay beside him
Till he died. Light streamed through the window
From the wide landscape of Downs and Weald
He loved to walk, upon brow and noble head,
Upon the book, his last contact with life:
The moon and *Cymbeline*, as he lay there dead.

Letter to Larkin

Dear Philip, I'm coming to my end too,
A decade and more older than you,
And your view of life just isn't true.
You made poetry out of sheer misery,
Out of the eldering man yourself,
Getting up in the night to piss
Half-drunk, after the hopelessness
Of the day's workload – the Toad.
Why not a day off, take the road
Out of the confines of Hull, your Hell,
To drink the beauty of landscape, sun on sea?
Instead of watching dawn creep up the curtain
I throw open the window and face sunrise,
Drink at the orange flame of the skies
Above the still and waiting ice-blue bay.
A moment later the light suffuses
Honey through the trees' meshed filigree,
And it is day . . .
Life isn't all misery
When out of it comes poetry.

The Years

How time has taken toll of their faces,
B.B. and Wystan from the Thirties to the Sixties.
Here is the composer of *Our Hunting Fathers,*
An unassuming boy, not yet certain of himself,
Cheeks unlined, head cocked forward,
Naif as a sparrow.
Wystan in the summer of '38
In Central Park, flaxen hair unruffled,
Pale face unblemished;
Not the innumerably creased and lined
Map of mummied skin of the Sixties,
The crevices of premature age
And saddened sick experience.
The innocent boy Ben has become
Something of a satyr by the Seventies,
Heavy face and worried frown,
Deep furrows in podgy cheeks,
Eyes narrowed with apprehension,
Himself an Aschenbach of his creation.

To David Cecil
on his Eightieth Birthday

———————

Eighty! – I cannot think that what you say
Can be – except that I am close to you,
Since the time when we were young: that day
When you arrived breathless up my stairs
In my remembered room with open view
Out over the Meadows in pale October sun –
Beginning of autumn term and of our lives
In that familiar city of our loves
And friendships: never to be so intense again.
Never such winged hours, every moment
Filled with sense of growth, honey from hives
Of mutual feeling and intellectual power.
Vivacity in every nerve, every word
That bubbled from your lips in the hurry
To express the thoughts that tumbled from your brain,
Helter-skelter, intelligible to me
Hardly, in my confused inadequacy!

What a mentor you were, and what a gift
For teaching: the inspiration I derived
From all you said and were! How much learned,
Returning only what little I had to give
In the encounter. Not much; but you were kind,
Forbearing to my immaturity
And naif optimism: wise to be
So patient of fanatic certainty,
When the fabric was falling about our very ears.
The years have told me since how right you were,
And taught me disenchantment and despair.

———————

Christ Church Meadows

Spring in the meadows and the warm air over me,
Elms and chestnuts put forth their shoots;
Over the river come cries of footballers,
While here the blackbirds practise their flutes.

A plane wings homeward from her journey
Into the eye of the setting sun;
Across the lady Montacute's Meadow
The shadows descend, and day is done.

Beyond the bounds of the gated city
Evening traffic makes a muted hum;
Under the trees the lovers are lying:
This is their moment: their hour will come.

Friends Gone Before

All the people who accompanied me
Through life are vanishing, one by one.
In the train we pass by Trematon,
Lived in by my friends the Caradons
No longer, with Sylvia the spirit gone.
Whither fled? She was the soul of the place,
Grande dame and gardener, hospitable,
Kindly and loving, generous with her plants.
And now St Germans, where Nellie presided at Port
Of the Eliots, and bravely held the fort,
The friend of Nancy Astor and Bernard Shaw.
Here is Nancy's Plymouth, never the same
Without her on the Hoe, playing her game
To the gallery, her bemused electorate.
Sometimes when in the city I step aside
Into St Andrew's to stand and remember her.
All three are gone, good women in their day,
For whom, alone on my way, I sigh, and pray.

Animals

Poor animals, I see a human soul
Looking out of their eyes
Struggling towards expression
Yet incapable of it
Unable to form words
The precious human gift
That so mesmerises them
Holds them in bond
Subjugates their will to ours
Creating for us an obligation
To return their loyalty
With an equal fidelity
And something of love
To the poor human soul
Looking out of faithful eyes –
Poor unfinished creatures:
Is it a soul lost
Or a soul unformed
That yet unspeaking
Speaks to us?

Innocent Heart

My Neddy delighted to be led to his field
After the day's long labour,
Unharnessed, bridle off,
Free.
Gate shut, he would canter and canter,
Roll over and over on his back,
Fart loudly, bray, let out
A prodigious long cock.
Then appeased, come up to the fence,
Ears forward, nuzzle me,
And happily accept an apple,
The day's work over.

A Lost Cat

'Only a woman's hair' –
Only a little cat:
All the sadness of life
For one or other is there.

He came to me late in life,
Willing to be my friend:
I thought to possess his heart
Right to the end.

No such hope now:
No answer to my call
Around house or garden,
The wilderness, or on the wall

Where he would often sit
With diamond eyes and wait,
To watch me up the path
And through the gate.

'Rake his little pathways out' –
Thomas Hardy speaks for me,
Rake out the leafy bed he made
In the elbow of a tree.

No scrambling down from nest
When at the door I call;
No eager answer to his friend –
Only the leaves that fall.

Cat-Fixation

_____

I suffer from a malady
The sophisticated call
Cat-fixation.

Wherever I go I find
Those winning ways
Await me.

Agate eyes, shell-whorl ears,
Gestures of instant beauty
And insinuation.

Loving to lie on whom they love
In ravishing attitudes,
Or feed by hand.

Expressions equally beguiling,
Acting 'wicked' or playing 'good'
In alternation.

With tail in rhythm waving –
No princess greets more sedately
From whatever station.

How could I endure to be without –
After despairing humans –
This consolation?

_____

My Last Cat

He was willing to be my companion;
When he saw me take up walking-stick
He was all agog to accompany me
Up into the wilderness –
Leaping along with frolic gaiety,
Pausing to play around a tree,
Then at the steps waiting to see
Which way I meant to step.
By the time I'd puffed up the slope
He'd be sitting pretty on the gate,
Pleased as puss at beating me.

Or couched at length along my bed,
Happy from warm night's sleep,
Would hiss at anyone's approach,
Fearing to be driven away from me.

Untamed out of the wild he came,
To find love and companionship
That rendered him perhaps too tame:
For, at the call of sex, one summer night
Over the western fields into the wood,
My friend, my beauty, whose coat
Would glisten in the flow of firelight
Silvery white and glossy black,
Into the perilous wild he went –
And never came back.

Out of Reach

I don't quite know why
They hate me so much:
Is it because I express such
Contempt for them?
For, as a friendly poet said,
They would destroy me if they could.
Why?
Is it that I
Am indestructible,
Straddling two worlds into which
They cannot reach?
Independent, irreducible,
Intolerant of mediocrity,
Never speaking their smooth speech,
Uncompromising,
Out of reach?

Bank Holiday

There has always been something withheld
In my relations with people, even with a friend
I now see, nearing life's end:
I could never give myself wholly –
Some inner inhibition,
Mistrust, or suspicion.
Perhaps I could not trust
Myself, inner insecurity
Forbade free flow.
And so
How much I have missed,
Determined to keep control, not cast
My bread upon the waters
To return an hundred fold,
Not trust to fate: what lost
In friendship, fruits of the spirit,
In mutual inspiration, by ruling out
Chance and obligation,
Bearing each other's burdens.
But chose to be solitary,
As now in this room so given to company,
Where not a soul's about
This May morning, all out
On Bank Holiday, and I alone –
Rose, blossom, sterile fruit,
Dust of mistrust.

The Wound

I received the wound or ever I was born:
The misused girl pregnant before her time
Going down the beach-road to the sea
To drown herself: arrested by her father
With that kind voice that called the cattle home,
Persuaded to return,
Protected from the whip of mother's tongue,
Turned out upon the roads,
Seared and exposed to scorn:
Now caught, an animal in the trap,
No way of escape but death,
Or an unwanted birth.
Hard to meet the accusing eye
Of friend or enemy, or passer-by,
With child to know the singular story
Of that obsessional haunted place,
The great vision of the guarded Mount.

That which was a closed book to me
Yet stamped a mark upon my brow,
The shreds and threads of human flesh
That wove together in a mother's womb.

Thus was the wound inherited,
Turned inward, away from the fact of life –
That never could the grown man
Come to terms with life and love.

Ambivalent

Androgynous, ambivalent, what
Kind of figure is that
For a man? Female of breast
And thigh, male muscle and back –
Nothing may be said to lack
Of masculine mind and brain;
Feminine intuition and temper,
Nothing in fact to hamper
Dual operation of spirit
Without tension now, or strain.

Safe

I closed the gates of my heart
In order not to be hurt
By the common course of life
Where at sight of a wound
Life will twist the knife
Not to let men know
Where they may place a blow
Carapace over the scar
Where one was wounded before
Grow the tissue hard
Ever keep watch and ward
The heart no more expose
Than inner bud of rose
To the inquisitive eye
I shut the gates – though I
Well know the price to pay
Confront it every day
A numb and withered life
Without love – but safe.

The Lost Leader

I could have been a leader –
I was meant for such,
But something came between
Something sometime said
No.
And when was that?
When disillusionment set in
Like plague or Spanish flu,
Or some creeping paralysis
Along the passionate veins
That eventually chilled
The warm heart's blood.

Fan Mail

You can be penniless –
That's nothing to do with me,
I do not know you, woman.
Why should you write to me
To you unknown
Bother me with your troubles?

But is it right that I
Should take no notice
Of your being penniless
No less?

I don't answer the letters
That people address
To me. Why should I?
And yet there reaches me a cry
Of distress,
And I
Not even reply.
No way to heaven.

The Ancient House

The night is full of noises, false alarms –
O preserve me from its harms –
A summer wasp awakes from winter sleep,
Drowsily explores the hanging at my head;
Bed creaks, door bangs at the far back,
A dull thud among rafters of the roof.
The ancient house, demure and coy by day,
Lovely and withdrawn, reserving her secret,
By night comes alive, to live once more
Her life of the past, respond to footfalls
Of former habitants, answer their muffled calls
For consolation and relief, in suffering,
The awakening of those born and those who died.
This secret life of stifled noises
Like scuttlings of mouse or rat
Warns me of my end in turn
Among all those.
Perhaps the footfall I hear upon the stair
Is my predestined murderer
Already there.

Chinese Dream

Why a Chinese dream last night?
Why that waiting figure between two others?
And I am bidden to behead the unknown person,
Take off the head neatly with a sword
At one stroke – like the executioner
Brought from Calais to take off
The head of Anne Boleyn.
'So little a neck', hands around her throat,
Rehearsing execution the night before.
I looked again at the unknown,
Not knowing why I was there,
Or who imposed on me this chore.
I realised I could not do it,
And in the night
Awoke in fright.

Finis

I am one of the defeated ones
I know now why I can no longer create,
Not age in me – Titian or Ranke
Could go on creating into their nineties:
It is the age itself that kills,
Kills all those who have the sensitivity
To recognise its horror.
Picasso expressed it all in *Guernica*,
As Eliot in *The Waste Land* –
The destruction of society,
The balanced equilibrium
Lost, for ever lost –
While time marches inexorably on
Perhaps to nuclear end.

The Soul

Beneath an earth–bank we call hedge
Two reapers rested that hot day,
In the golden stubble field
Above the blue extended bay.

There they slumbered, after work
From early morn until the noon . . .
A grey mist rose above the sea,
Turned the air to cold; and soon

The younger of them now awoke,
Looked across at his friend's head:
A white moth fluttered from his mouth,
And then he knew that he was dead.

The Chosen

———————

'You have been good to me.'
– 'Yes I have. You have been tried in the fire
And saved from burning.'
'But why was I so tried?'
'I do not know. Perhaps before
I took particular note of you.
And named you one
Of the Chosen.'

———————

The Hand

———————

What hand is it that was held over me
Which I ungrateful failed to recognise?
Often at night I think of those dark streets,
Dark and dangerous off Third Avenue
Waiting, waiting for someone to turn up –
Might be thug, mugger, murderer –
For ever unsatisfied, insatiable of life.
And strangely at the midnight hour
Silence and vacuity – nobody came.
When what encounter might have been
To meet one's fate, a strangled body
Anonymous beside a corner wall.
What risks taken, dangers to have survived,
Unrealised then, recognised only now
Nearing life's end, perhaps a peaceful close
Granted at last by that invisible Hand.

———————

The Garden

I can't face it that I have to die
I have lived so long it must come soon
But how or when, wherefore or why
One day rather than another,
By day or night, sunlight or moon:
Wouldn't it be happier in the garden,
No-one around, one hot summer noon,
The buzzing of bees, coloured butterflies
Fluttering amid the buddleias
Blue sky overhead, a white cloud in the west
And I lying quiet on the ground
Cool green leaves to cover my face
In that beloved familiar place –
Let it be in the garden, if it might be –
In my ears the dying surf of the sea.

The Veil

The finger of God, the finger of God –
Is He reaching out to me, I wonder?
I cannot tell. I only know
I am unworthy
I have not yet achieved
Transparency
To myself – I cannot see
My way - I am blind
I can only feel
What is behind
The veil.

Death

O death, when will it come?
I am afraid to think
When heart's dry, mind dumb,
And I have only to drink
The ultimate dark.

O death, when will it be
That I have life to leave,
And all that I have loved
Over the years to grieve:
Places, creatures, work.